THE 10 KEYS TO SUCCESS

THE 10 KEYS TO SUCCESS

John Bird

LARGE
PRINT

First published in 2008 by
Vermilion, an imprint of
Ebury Publishing
This Large Print edition published
2008 by BBC Audiobooks by
arrangement with
Ebury Press

ISBN 978 1 405 62235 6

Quick Reads™ used under licence.

British Library Cataloguing in Publication Data available

Printed and bound in Great Britain by
CPI Antony Rowe, Chippenham, Wiltshire

Contents

Chapter One

Be the Best *You* Can Be

I have very little time for those books that contain mumbo jumbo like, 'You can be anything you want. You just have to believe.' Well, excuse me for throwing cold water over your dreams, but I think we all know that is utter rubbish. You may as well say that just wishing for a million pounds will deliver it. The sad thing is there are people who believe this. They read these so-called positive thinking books that tell them they only have to think it and they will have it. Now, seriously, how do you think that's going to happen?

Sure, there are those few people who seem to rise to dizzy heights despite having the odds stacked against them, but the reason we read about them is because they are special. The rest of us must learn to work with what we've got. I'm not saying that your life is decided for you. I just think we all have to come to terms with our own talents and skills, and figure out what we can do with them. It may not be possible to be *anything* you want but it is possible to become *something.*

What Can You Do in the Real World?

We have all seen those talent shows on TV where people who can't sing a note think that they can do it very well. All that happens is that they look foolish. You watch them and you start to wonder why they are doing it, when they could be putting their energies into something else. Apart from the ones who are really a bit mad, it's obvious that many of them have not been honest with themselves. You can see them thinking, 'Anyone can do it, so why can't it be me?' Well, sure, anyone can do it, but you need to be able to sing first. And then you need to have that thing called star quality. Frankly speaking, those two things alone mean that very few people can do it. The rest are living in a dream world.

My point is that you can have all the dreams you want, but you need to put something towards those dreams to make them work. The engine won't go if you don't put the right fuel into it. Have you got that fuel? For example, if you want to run a café you need to know what people eat and how to make it. You need to know how to draw up a budget. You need some money to put towards it. You need the freedom to work all the hours God sends. You need to like people because it's a people business. And then you need to put it all together, and be prepared not to make any real money for maybe a year. If you have spent the past

25 years working in an office for someone else, this kind of move will be a big shock. It is not an impossible dream but it means you need to be honest with yourself.

What are you aiming for? You might be thinking about moving to another country, changing your job or even improving your social skills. Get a piece of paper. At the top of the page write down your aim. Let's say it's a career change. You might even know what you'd like to do. Perhaps you'd like to work in the City, and you know you need to get some sort of qualification in finance. You have seen that there are many courses on offer. So now you need to figure out how to fit that into your current life, because you're going to have to juggle both things for a while.

On one side of the page write down the things in your life that will help you make this happen. For instance, you might have help from your family, a strong desire to do the course and a college close by. Those are strengths. But on the other side you will need to write down weak points. These might include the fact that you have not studied for some time, and that you will find it hard to make time to study, even with family support. Once you have done this, you need to figure out how you can improve those weak points and maybe even get rid of them. Perhaps you could start work earlier one day so you can get to your course on time. It's a bit like trying to make the pieces of a jigsaw fit together, and you need to think it through.

It is only when you have a firm idea of what you want to do that you can work towards it. Say you want to live in the country. If you think, 'I want to move out of London at some point,' you are less likely to achieve it. This is because 'moving out of London at some point' is not a firm goal. It is too big and airy fairy. You need to think about where you will live and how you will live. In the country? In a house? Are you going to sell your house? Are you going to rent one? What work will you do? The more you narrow down your idea into something clear, the more likely you are to work out whether you can do it. Otherwise I reckon you're just playing at it.

Work Your Way Up

If you've been honest about your skills and you have a pretty solid idea of what you want, what happens next? Well, you need to start somewhere and that means starting small. When I wanted to move out of a life of poor jobs, my first aim was to keep out of trouble. When I had managed to do that for a few years I was pleased with myself. 'Goodness,' I thought, 'I can change.' That made me feel that something new was possible.

Then I wanted to learn a skill. I wanted to learn about printing. It was something I'd always been interested in. So I applied for a job and worked my way around the printing firm, learning everything I could. I did it well and that made me feel I could take another, bigger step. After a few years, I wanted to work for myself, because I felt that working for other people was wasting all my new skills. I was ready for it because I had moved slowly. I decided I wanted to use all the stuff I knew and produce a magazine. My friend Gordon Roddick, who founded the Body Shop with his wife Anita, had seen street papers in New York. He knew about my interest in helping the homeless and told me about this idea. He wasn't giving it to me on a plate. He was saying, look, here is a good step for you if you can take it.

How *The Big Issue* Works

Homeless people apply to become vendors and sell *The Big Issue*. We ask them to sign a code of conduct that sets out how we expect them to behave while they are on the street selling the magazine. We give them 10 free magazines to start them off. After that they only get what they can pay for, because looking after money is part of what we want them to learn. We run a bank to help them put money by. The idea is to give people 'a hand up, not a hand-out', and help them earn a living so we hope they can go on to something bigger and better.

We are a business, but our aim is not to make money for its own sake. We invest our profits into our charity, The Big Issue Foundation.

I was able to move onwards not by aiming for the top job, but by doing one thing at a time. I also stuck to a path. For example, I didn't decide that after being a printer I wanted to manage a record shop. You can't go firing in all directions. You have to stick to the same area, so that you can take what you have learned with you. Printing was a natural stepping stone for publishing. Even when I started *The Big Issue*, I did not think of myself as the 'boss'. I was simply the guy who was setting it up. Being the leader only becomes your job because you have done all the other jobs. You have to earn it. By the way, I am still not as good as I could be. I have always been very bad at organisation and small details. So I have spent a lot of time working on that weakness, because I know it matters when you do what I do.

If someone's dream was to move to Spain, they could start making it happen by working on their weak points. They might have debts and not be able to speak Spanish. It makes sense that, while they are working to clear their debts, they could also be learning Spanish. Now they might say, 'God, that will take forever.' But as the months pass their debt will lessen and their Spanish will improve. By the time two years is up, they will be in a very good position to make their move. See how things can come together?

Limits Can Be Overcome

Life is about taking steps that move you forwards. You don't have to worry about going forwards quickly. What matters is that you are moving and that you keep moving until you hit your limits. By that point you will have gained so much more confidence in what you are doing that you will most likely find a way to move beyond those limits. That is how most people work. Believe me, it is not about being a super brain most of the time.

Remember

- You can't be anything you want. But you can be something.
- Take an honest look at your strengths and weak points.
- Decide the best way to use your strengths and how to make them even stronger.
- Decide which weak points you can turn into strengths and which ones you can do nothing about.
- Work with what you have instead of wishing for what you can't have or what someone else has got.
- We can all do something but we have to find it. You will know when you find it because it will feel right for you.

Chapter Two

Fight for Your Optimism
Every Day

Imagine saying to someone, 'Look Jane, I don't think you should go on holiday because you don't know if you will enjoy it.' Or, 'My advice to you Lisa is not to have a family. You never know, they may all end up in prison or as prostitutes in some foreign city.' 'John,' you say, 'nobody would ever say that.' Sorry, but they do. That is exactly what people are saying when they ask you, 'Are you sure your idea will work?' And I suspect it's also what you have found yourself saying to other people.

The day I told a member of my family that I was going to start a street paper for homeless people his reply was classic: 'Well, how do you know it's going to work?' I didn't *know* it was going to work. How could I predict the future? But I was sure as hell going to give it a shot. Everything we do, every step we take, is because we believe it is worth doing. We don't always know if we will end up where we want to be, but we have to give it a try. Even before we do that, we have to fight for our light and keep fighting for it. Because there will always be people who say, 'I don't think that will work.'

Don't Let Them Get You Down

At the moment I am looking out of a window at a small pond. A family of moorhens lives in a cluster of reeds on the pond. Each morning I am amazed when I see their fluffy little chicks come out, bobbing around, dipping their beaks in the water. In previous years, crows have taken the chicks and eaten them. They have been attacked by roaming foxes. Yet the mother and father still get on with raising their chicks into adults. Of course they are driven by nature, but even so it is a great example of standing up against the world. I can't help feeling that there are too many people in the world who are standing there ready to say, 'The crows will have you!' And it's this you have to fight against.

We live in a world where people are ready to tell you that all is doom and gloom, even if it isn't. The news media thrive on 'scare' stories. These make me angry. Coffee drinkers are supposed to be at greater risk of bladder cancer and less risk of liver and colon cancer. We are told not to fly, take trains or drive cars. And those of us with children should wrap them up in cotton wool and leave them there until they are 18 years old, because it seems life is far too nasty for them. In time all these things will be replaced by other 'scare' stories. Doesn't that tell you something is not quite right?

We have to be careful not to fall under the spell of what we read and hear. To keep your sanity in this crazy world you need to stay focused on your own life. When you read or hear these things, don't give them a home in your brain. Instead, bear in mind that you still have a life to get on with as best you can, just like millions of other people. Think of the great things that people like you have done. Yes, normal people like you. I am always impressed by people who go that extra mile for their fellow human beings. They help to blow holes in our cynical world that seems to put a downer on everything.

- Back in the early days of *The Big Issue*, a young couple got married. They decided they wanted to do something really useful at the wedding. They didn't want presents. They didn't even want flowers. Instead, they wanted their guests to give some money to *The Big Issue*. I was amazed, because I would have thought that the one day when you wanted to be spoilt was your wedding day.

- Every Saturday morning a hairdresser would get up and travel to London to *The Big Issue* office. She cut hair from 9 a.m. until we closed in the afternoon. The hair was no ordinary hair. It was the hair of people with health problems. She was cutting hair to help the homeless to help themselves. She was a hardworking woman who decided she wanted to do something for others.

- A young woman I know meets a homeless person once a week for an evening. They talk. They swap knowledge. The young woman teaches the homeless young woman French. The homeless young woman teaches the other young woman maths. They work together. They overcome prejudice. They are helping each other towards a useful life.

I meet hundreds of people a year who do not stand idly by. All of these people had to fight for their optimism every minute of the day. Don't think it came any easier to them.

Optimism does not mean you won't worry. But there are different kinds of worry. There is the kind of worry that leaves your brain numb, where you sit on the couch and do nothing and just sink into despair. And then there is good worry, when just thinking about doing something new gets you all tense and excited. And that's normal. Once you start what you want to do, whether it's build a shed or go and visit someone you haven't seen in 30 years, that worry will start to calm down. Believe me, it will.

Stop Looking for Approval from Others

Just because you want to do something doesn't mean the rest of the world shares your delight. Seeking approval from other people might seem like a positive thing to do at the start. You know how it works. You have an idea. Let's say you want to go back to study part-time. You are both excited and a bit scared by the idea, since you haven't done any study since school. So you go and ask some people. What you are hoping is that they will say exactly what you want to hear. 'Wow, what a great idea.' Instead they tell you it is a dream, a waste of time and that it will stress you out and ruin your life. So then you start thinking that maybe it is not such a good idea.

And that, in a nutshell, is the problem with seeking approval.

Many of us are what I like to call approval 'addicts'. We just can't get off our bums and do anything unless we get the nod from others. This addiction, like all other addictions, can only result in a life that is wasted. 'But John,' you say, 'isn't it normal to want others to agree with you?' I will say that it is a natural human urge, but sometimes you have to disagree and go your own way.

I think it's safe to say that approval addicts get nowhere. They certainly don't become leaders. That's because they don't own their idea. Instead, they wait for other people to let them know what they can do. This just sounds dumb and pathetic to me. Are you so desperate to do what other people want that you would jump off a cliff if they told you to? Of course not. So why are you basing your life choices on what they think?

I'm now going to say something that might upset more than a few people. Do you think the people closest to you have your best interests at heart? Are they really thinking of your needs and desires? They're not. It is very hard for humans, especially loved ones, to say things that are based purely on fact. That's because they will bring their own experience into play—their own lost dreams, their personal failures and their jealousy. So when you ask them for their opinion, you are getting a lot of baggage.

Starting *The Big Issue* was based on an optimism that some people saw as a daydream. Many people around me pointed out that it would not work. They said I was the wrong person. I had been involved in many failures in my life. I was too disorganised. I was unreliable. You could say that these views were not so far wrong. On the other hand, why did my past have to decide my future? I don't believe people don't change. They do. And I am living proof of that.

My childhood was almost invented to destroy me, to make me a nasty, selfish, aggressive man. My parents lived in a slum in Notting Hill, London. I was the third of six children. My parents did not pay the rent. They did not feed us properly because they really did not know how to be parents. Cigarettes and drink were more important than food. It was a violent world where I saw my father beat my mother. It was no surprise that we kids ended up in a home when our parents were made homeless. I spent my youth getting in trouble with the police through truancy, stealing and violence. I spent time in prison. I was dishonest, lazy and useless. Today, all that is behind me. I learned how to take lessons from my past and use them for a better future.

When I thought about starting

The Big Issue, I was ready to make a go of something. Much of what had happened in my past had brought me to the point where I was ready to start a magazine. Through jobs I'd had, I'd taught myself how to print and design a magazine. I knew how to put articles together. I understood how to get people to write for you and how to create a balanced magazine. So I wasn't just talking out of my you-know-where. I had based my dream on something that I was able to do in practical terms. It wasn't as if I'd said, 'I'm going to invent a space rocket.'

I also had good people to help me. I had people who knew how to raise money and where to look for it, people to design the magazine and people who knew how to write. What I didn't have at that early stage was a strong relationship with the homeless community, but I knew I would get that as we went on. That's another point worth noting. If you want to start something, you can't wait for everything to be in place. You have to start somewhere. It's a mixture of being prepared enough, but not putting it off until you think it's all perfect.

You Can't Build on Daydreams

I want to make the point here that my optimism had real foundations. It may not have been built on concrete but it was solid in every way. It was about having a clear direction, and being organised and prepared. So my optimism was about looking out at the world and being upbeat about what could be done. I didn't set myself up to fail. Optimism has to be based firmly on the real world, not an ideal world that has yet to happen.

Most of all, optimism is something you have to fight for every day. And some days it won't come easily, which is fine. You will have days when you feel you have sunk a little, and then you will have others when you bounce back. Hopefully, if you have a plan and believe in it, you will ride this roller coaster and come out of it the right way at the end. In many ways your success depends on your ability to direct your emotions and feelings the right way. The practical stuff takes far less energy. But turning your mind around when it is telling you it can't see the road ahead is tough. Just remember, it's not a problem. It's part of your journey to success.

Remember

- Get a clear idea of what matters to you. Ignore the negative voices.
- Stop looking for approval from others, even those close to you.
- Live in the real world—be

practical about what you can do.
- Don't confuse daydreams with optimism—they are not the same thing.
- Fight and keep fighting for your optimism every day. Never give up.

Chapter Three

Don't Wait for the Perfect Time to Start

I tend to get involved in things in a way that some people would see as ill-prepared. But it's not. It's a risk I'm prepared to take. Whether you are looking to start a self-improvement programme or get your finances in order, there is no perfect time. Business people who have had success don't wait for the perfect time to start something. Sure, they will be thoughtful about having the right skills and people to kick off with, but they also know that if they wait too long, someone else will come along under their nose. So what they do is jump in and solve problems as they come up.

It is very rare that the people, money, emotions, skills and even the planets—if you believe in that sort of thing—come together exactly when you want them to. Sometimes you just have to go with what you have.

I Started at the 'Wrong' Time

In 1991 the economy was in a bad place. In business terms, money was tight and people were not looking to invest in new things. We knew it was not a good time to start anything, let alone something charity-based. People were only interested in their own survival. So the idea of *The Big Issue*, a social business that relies on money from the general public, couldn't have come at a worse time. When money is scarce and people don't want to spend, it affects everything. As well as street sales, we needed advertisers to buy space in *The Big Issue* and bring in money. However, like everyone else, they were also not spending.

We felt that we still had to do it. We had a solid idea and, even more important, fire in our bellies. Gordon Roddick, our sponsor, agreed. There was no time to waste. Sure, we were not big on experience or some of the skills we needed, but we felt we could make up for that by sheer hard work. We were not going to let things get in our way. Boy, did we have people telling us what to do, or rather what not to do. They said we were out of touch. That people would not support a new charity at a time like this. They said the mood out there was wrong because people were not interested in helping anyone. Then they said that our idea—where the poor would be encouraged to sell the magazine and help themselves—sounded too much like the views of Maggie Thatcher, whom a lot of people did not like at the time.

Looking back, I now know that, no matter when you decide to make a change, there will always be people who tell you it is stupid, wrong or foolish. 'Why do you want to change jobs when you already have a good one?' 'What are you doing using your savings to market a new product?' 'Why do you want to move out of London? It's the wrong time.'

When you hear people say things like this, you need to take it with a pinch of salt. Much of the time they will say it because they are jealous of you and your courage. They will tell themselves that risk is stupid, that it will only lead to something bad and mess up their lives. So then you come along, all excited and full of energy about doing something new, and they are not pleased. Because they do not want to leave their comfort zone, the idea of you doing so is very scary. It reminds them that they have dreams they want to follow, dreams they don't have the courage or guts to chase.

So what I would say is yes, do

listen to advice, but restrict the people you listen to. You want to talk to people who understand what you're trying to do and why, people who won't let their emotions interfere in your decision. You should be looking for people who calmly point out the strengths and weaknesses you have and what to watch out for. In fact, if you ask people for advice it's a good idea to say, 'What I want from you is some idea of what you think my biggest obstacle will be and how I might get over that.' In that way you are less likely to get caught up in endless discussions that go nowhere.

Improve as You Go Along

Life is about learning to adapt and adopt as you progress. There is a story about a university in Texas that built two computers. One was made up of the best of all possible parts.

The other was made of rejected parts. Both worked very well. The message here is that it doesn't have to be perfect to succeed. Sure, you can work at making it better. That's exactly what we did with *The Big Issue*. We set it up as best we could and transformed it as we went along.

For example, I didn't have the perfect team. It's like a relationship. You could meet someone and think, 'Yes, I like them,' and decide that you will go on seeing them. Or you could meet them and think, 'They are nice but maybe I should look for someone better.' The point is that you have to see how you get on with people, or you will be forever looking. I believed we would find the best team as we went along.

One of the first people I employed was a great guitarist. He had no experience in publishing or of starting a magazine. He had never worked with homeless people or really thought about them and their problems. But he had his feet on the ground. He was a kind human being with a good sense of humour. He had vision and ideas and I felt he would learn very quickly. He was also short of cash and needed to work, a fact which drove both of us. We learned a hell of a lot as we went along. There is no better way to pick up the skills you need.

You also have to trust your judgement. After all, at this stage, what else do you have? There was another man I met in the early days, more a boy than a man. He had just left public school and had this posh accent. As I often did, I interviewed him in the pub. Other members of the team were sitting around drinking. I knew they thought he would not get the job. They didn't like him. However, the more I talked to him the more I became convinced that he needed to be given a chance. He was a good thinker. And he would probably prove to be a good writer. Meanwhile, the others were making signals to me that I should not give him any more time. I disagreed and decided to take him on. He became our best writer.

A woman I know threw in her job in order to start a small shop. She was advised against it. It was the wrong time. It was the wrong city. There were so many things wrong with the whole idea that she should have given up. But she did not. She opened the shop and now, five years later, she sells on the internet, is looking at another shop and is a big wholesale supplier. This woman realised that the right time would never exist and that there really was no time like the present.

Get Ready to Leave Your Comfort Zone

Have you watched those comedy shows where comics have to make up a speech or act something out without any preparation? These men and women are really going out of their comfort zone. You might say, 'But it's what they do all the time.' Nonsense. Getting up to perform without a script is very different to doing it with one. These people do it on purpose to stretch themselves, to see how good they really are and even to frighten themselves. There is a real rush of blood that comes from stepping outside your place of comfort.

The fact is that all success lies out of your comfort zone. The need to climb over your own personal fence comes when you realise you are not getting what you need inside it. So how do you know that? Simple. When you reach a place where you are more and more unhappy with your life, you have to get out of your comfort zone.

There is a quote that goes, 'If you keep doing what you've always done then you'll keep getting what you've always got.' If you could just do what you've been doing for years to get what you want, you would. My point is that, if you want to change something in your life, you have NO CHOICE but to move out of your comfort zone. A comic may re-use old material because they know it works. True, it will work for a while, maybe even for a very long time. But time moves on and things change. Sooner or later most of us have to change direction. It can be very difficult to make a shift in your life, especially if you have little money. You might not have all the choices in the world, but you still have some.

Remember

- There is often no right time to start something but you need to start anyway.
- As long as you are aware there

are good and bad sides to everything, it is not foolish to jump into something. Just be prepared.

- Don't aim to be perfect straight away. Start, and improve as you go along.
- Be prepared to trust your own judgement because that is all you have.
- It's all right to feel scared, as long as that doesn't stop you acting.
- Accept that sometimes you will have to change the way you have always done things.

Chapter Four

Make Sure Your Passion *is* Practical

This really follows on from what I said in the first chapter about daydreams. It applies even more to you if you have some idea of 'helping' people. I think it's great that people are becoming more interested in what is going on around them and in helping others. I think it's great that more young people have ideals that go beyond making money. And I think it's great that they are willing to go out on a limb to make things happen.

What worries me are misplaced ideals, where people haven't thought about how things will work in a practical way. Then they get upset when nobody listens to them. It's wonderful to have visions of something better for you, your family, your community or the world. But you need to have thought about how you can make them work in real life. When I came up with my views on what I would do to change homelessness, I knew I had to stand back and look at it with a clear eye. For example, I couldn't allow my own experiences on the streets to affect things in an emotional way. You can't be *emotional* when you want to make changes in society. You have to look at the facts and be very practical. I think the fact that I can put my own past behind me, while understanding the homeless, has helped me see things clearly and succeed with *The Big Issue*.

Do it for the Right Reasons

We often make changes in our lives because something has jolted us out of our normal way of thinking. For example, I know that many people decide that their lives would be better served if they worked for charities. This is something they often do after they have been through a crisis.

The wonderful, late Jane Tomlinson managed to work for charity for five years despite having breast cancer. She is an example of someone who found a direction in life because her own life changed radically. She succeeded not by being emotional about her illness, but by getting out there and showing that people like her still had a life to live and needed to be helped. Jane was also fortunate that her husband and family understood why she chose to go running and push herself physically where other cancer patients would be trying to preserve their energy. The more out-of-the-ordinary your direction in life, the more you will need to believe in yourself and be optimistic about your chances of success. That's because it may be hard to find people who share your passion. Equally, some people may think you are a bit mad.

In my own case, I know that many people think I have strong ideals. The fact is, yes, I do have dreams for a better world, but I don't let those views get in the way of what can and cannot be done in real life. I have learned those lessons. I started *The Big Issue* because I wanted to pay my mortgage. I was working as a printer and was sick of not having enough money, and I had certain beliefs about the way the homeless were dealt with. The point is I didn't start *The Big Issue* because I'm a soft, caring person who wants to hug the homeless. I felt for them, but I also felt that I could show them and the rest of the world a better way forward.

It's easy to say now, but back then I had no idea if anyone would listen to me. My ideas were so at odds with the way the government and charities treated the homeless. Their view was that it was all about shelter and providing places to sleep, such as hostels. But when I looked hard at the problem I saw something else. Many of the people on the streets were not well. In fact, they were very ill. They had problems with drink and drugs and did not know how to control them. They needed help with mental health problems. They also needed to help themselves. That's when the idea of *The Big Issue* came to life. It would be a magazine they could sell that would give them a reason in life to get up. They would earn money from each issue they sold. When we started, people were very unsure about it. That included the homeless themselves. But we gradually won them over and many other people besides.

Make Other People Believe

People often think that just because they have a good idea, everyone else will see it that way. I wish I could tell you it was that easy. The fact is that, even if you have the best idea in the world, people may not buy it. Think about JK Rowling who created the Harry Potter books. She was rejected by several publishers before one took a risk on her. The point is that you must put a lot of effort into selling your idea. Don't just think, 'But it's so good, why can't they see it?' They can't see it because they're not you, so what you have to do is show them, step by step, what you are seeing.

Here's a funny thing. The more you believe in your idea, the better you will be able to sell it. It will show in your face and your body language. You will speak in a more confident voice and you will even walk tall. And the more you do that, the more you will make others wonder, 'What if he has something? He sounds confident. Maybe I should listen?'

When you truly believe in what you are doing, you can convince people even when things are bad. I recall one time when a newspaper was about to expose one of our vendors. Apparently he was earning £1500 a week selling *The Big Issue*. That's what he told everyone who would listen. He had been going into pubs boasting. He was going to destroy our reputation. According to some of our staff it was going to be the beginning of the end. So far we had never had any bad press and this was very bad news. It was our first big test of whether we had public confidence.

I was sure that we could survive and turn it to our advantage. I knew that we were in the right, and I had no reason to defend my position. So I went off and did interviews with the press in a very positive way. I stuck to the facts. I told the journalists that, given the amount of money the homeless earned from selling *The Big Issue*, there was no way on earth someone could earn such a sum. They would have to put in at least 14 hours a day! This argument made sense to them. I also told them about how homeless people can exaggerate. I kept my cool. I pointed out how it was possible that the average vendor made just enough to keep themselves in body and soul. They listened and they realised I was telling the truth. It was a tough moment.

Learn to Sell Yourself

To get someone to believe in your dreams, your ideas or indeed in you, you need to make them feel that if they don't listen they might be missing out on something. Even if you have some questions that you haven't quite answered yourself—

which you will—you have to sound like you have it worked out 100 per cent. When I started *The Big Issue* I did not have everything worked out. Not the small details. Not who would do all the writing. Not how we would show the homeless that this was good for them. But what I did have was a vision that sounded strong and exciting, and that I truly believed in from the bottom of my heart. Even more important, I had thought about how practical it was. As I said earlier, it's one thing to have a dream, but don't let your vision of a better world blind you to the nuts and bolts of making something happen.

I knew I had something good to offer. I just had to work hard to make sure others understood it. That meant that I had to shake them up. I had to make them look beyond the normal ways of helping the homeless. It was almost as if the more I got them to believe me, the less they hung on to their old beliefs.

One of the most common reasons for not getting what you want is not asking for it in the right way. Say you have an idea about how things could be improved at your office. It is a good idea and makes sense. But now you need to convince your boss. The first thing you have to think about is what you want to happen when you speak to him. Let's say that you think the office should be less formal. You think it might make people more creative. Now, what will you do if it doesn't happen? Will you get upset? Will you take it personally? Or will you just accept it? Now think about how you will approach your boss. You could just go and meet with him yourself and state your idea. You could write it down and send it to him so he can read it before you meet. Or you could try and rally support by sending the idea to everyone in the office.

What are the risks of each

approach and where is the least risk? How much risk do you want to take? You see, the more you prepare for every possible reaction, the better your chances of getting a good outcome for yourself. The person who goes to the bank manager to ask for a loan needs to be ready to answer all sorts of questions. It's not enough to say, 'I need the money to go back to school.' You need to show the bank that you have a vision for yourself, for a better life and how it will benefit you in the end. That is what will make them invest in you.

When business people sit down together to make a deal, they rarely do so without thinking about what the other person might say. They will have spent time before a meeting working out what sort of response they will get to their ideas. Then they will think about how they will deal with that. And that's what gives them confidence, the kind of confidence that makes others believe in them.

Remember

- It's great to have big visions but they have to be workable and real.
- Just because you think it's great, doesn't mean everyone else will.
- The more different or unusual your ideas are, the harder you will have to work to sell them.
- The more you believe in your idea and have thought about it, the better you can sell it to others.
- If you are confident, people will be more likely to believe in you.
- Learn how to ask for things in the way that is most likely to achieve the best results.

Chapter Five

Start with the Small Steps

A big part of staying positive and focused, no matter what you want to do, is getting some quick wins under your belt. Doing this means you have to aim small. 'Hang on, John,' you're thinking, 'what about all those self-help books that tell me to aim really high?' Well, if I write what I really think about some of those books, they won't put it in, so I'll just say that it sounds good on paper but in real life that's not how things work.

If you set your sights too high from the outset, you are only setting yourself up to fail. You must have your eye on the prize, of course, but you must also realise that the big prize only comes after lots and lots of small steps. Think about the steps involved in applying for a job. You see the ad and decide to write an application. You send off the application and wait. You get an interview but it might be the first of two or three. If you get through those, you then give references. It's all a series of steps, but if you're smart you don't think about the whole thing at the beginning. You just think about getting your application seen, so you try and focus on writing a really good one.

If I start something with the hardest task, I will quickly wear myself out. You need to start with things you know you can do with a minimum of effort. Working this way means that you don't fall at the first hurdle, and that will give you more confidence. Work on today and leave tomorrow until the time comes.

Go for the Quick Wins First

When I started *The Big Issue* the first thing I did was appoint a man who was an all-rounder. He could write well enough. He could talk to the police. He could talk to the homeless. He could look after himself. Actually, he was a bit like me, but more polite and presentable than I was in 1991! I knew that we would soon need to get other people to do much of the editorial work, and the working with the homeless, so I picked someone reliable, hardworking and positive. He understood what the process of setting up a magazine was likely to be. But he also knew that we needed to get moving with some basic steps.

From the beginning I refused to surround myself with negative people, no matter how talented they were. I did not seek someone from the top of the pile, the biggest, strongest, most well-educated type of person. I took on someone who liked what he saw and was prepared to muck in. I knew he would help us gain those early, small successes that we needed to feel good about the project. He helped me map out the structure of the business. He left after his work was done, but that didn't matter because he'd set us on our way.

Then I concentrated on the design and feel of the magazine because I knew something about that end of the business. Doing that meant I had more chance of making progress than if, for example, I'd jumped straight in and tried to figure out how to get the homeless community on board. With the 'dummies' of the magazine ready, the idea of *The Big Issue* started to become real. We had layouts, designed pages of the magazine, that we could actually pick up and hold in our hands. It looked as though we had more of a business than we thought we would. At that point our little team started to get very excited. We had started. We were on our way!

Before we knew it, we had a team of people who, like me, could turn their hands to many different areas. We then looked at getting our first articles. Of course I wanted the best articles, written by the best people. I wanted them to be sparkling and exciting so that people would take notice. But I couldn't think about that. I had to have stuff written. So, rather than beat myself up about getting award-winning, big-name writers and interviews, I decided I needed to get *something*. I went to people I knew, people who wrote, and asked them to produce something for me. It was the simplest route, the route that would give me and the team the confidence that our product was coming together. What I did there was take the smart road. It wasn't the most perfect road, but it meant I got started.

Now, some of you with dreams of starting a magazine or writing a book might argue that settling for *just something* is a bit like settling for defeat. My question to you is, where exactly are you going to start then? And how will you know when you have the perfect start? By getting something down on paper, you have something to discuss and improve. Waiting for divine words from God or the most perfect moment is not going to help you get anywhere. You need to get in there and make something happen.

You Don't Need to Prove Yourself to Anybody

Don't take the hardest task first to prove how tough or commanding you are. Likewise, taking on the easier steps first doesn't make you a lesser person.

This works when you're trying to

win people over in meetings as well. If you try to argue for the big stuff straight away, you're likely to get people offside and make a difficult situation worse. Start by asking them the easy questions, the ones they can answer, and then things will be a lot smoother.

The easy prizes in starting *The Big Issue* fell like low-hanging fruit. Things just seemed to figure themselves out. And when it got a little more difficult we were confident and clever enough to handle it. When our magazines were being robbed by homeless people, we didn't enter into a deep debate about honesty and integrity. For people with damaged backgrounds it would have been meaningless. Instead, we worked out that we could pay the biggest and heaviest of the homeless to help us stop the others getting out of line. Soon we had homeless people who lined up quietly to buy the paper when only a few months before they had been very aggressive.

The problems never stopped, of course. If you start a business, they never do. But I stuck to my attitude of taking on the things I could handle. After about nine months of publication, Gordon Roddick, our sponsor, took me into a pub and said, 'I'm losing £25K a month on your *Big Issue*. I'll give you three months to sort it out. By September you become profitable, or I'll pull out.'

When I got back to the office and told the others, they were very worried. I, on the other hand, was calm. That night I sat over a piece of paper and worked out my plan. I would hit the soft parts first. I would negotiate with another printer. I would change the size of the paper and cut production costs by about 40 per cent. I would change the quality of the paper it was printed on. Then I would make us a fortnightly magazine rather than a monthly. This meant we would have two products a month to sell. Those were the easy bits. But there was still work to do. The tough stuff. I had to lay off some people, 10 in all. I felt confident doing it, though, because I had been working up to it and now it seemed the right thing to do.

I left the hardest thing until last. I doubled the price at which the homeless bought the magazine from us, from 10p to 20p. By the end of the three months the £25K loss had become a £1K monthly profit.

The lesson of paying attention to the small details is something that huge organisations forget at their peril. I went into a hospital with my pregnant wife. We stood in a room full of vast amounts of expensive, state-of-the-art medical equipment. A nurse came up and started asking us questions. She then realised that she needed to make a note of what we were telling her. She had the pen but she didn't have the paper. There was no paper nearby. So she took a paper towel and wrote on it. That small detail sums up the state of our health service. It has lost touch with the people, with the little things that matter.

On the other hand, it doesn't pay to get carried away with the small things when they don't matter. I did that and lost the best job I thought a printer could have. I had always wanted to be the printer for a college or a university. I believed that the stuff I printed would be more interesting. Since I always read what I printed, this was important to me. I had an interview at the London School of Economics and did very well indeed. The panel were smiling. Then they asked me if I had any questions. So I asked where I could lock up my bike. Well, as you can imagine this did me no favours, since it meant that these important people had to spend time discussing my bike. I knew as soon as I left the room that the little thing had tripped me up. They had seen a side of me they should not have seen. Of course, I missed out on the job.

Remember

- Go for the easy wins first.
- Get the basics right and you can build on them.
- Put perfection to one side. Just think about improving bit by bit.
- Work on today and leave tomorrow until it comes.
- Even big business is built on small details.
- Doing the easy stuff first doesn't make you stupid. It makes you smart and builds confidence for the harder stuff later on.

Chapter Six

Be Prepared to Go the Distance

Do you want to run in the race? Or do you want to win it? Anyone can come up with a grand plan and talk about it. Very few people will be able to put it into action, and fewer still will stick with it until the end. If there is one thing that you can learn from all those reality shows where people try to set up restaurants or renovate houses, it's that not everybody has the heart for a long battle. In fact, it's as plain as day that some of those people shouldn't even bother turning up because they are not for real.

There are far too many people around who are lying to themselves. They talk about what they can do but they never do anything. If you're not prepared to put the work in, no idea will ever be anything more than a dream, no matter how good it is. You have to be prepared to put in the hard miles and not give up. You have to commit and not think of quitting when it gets too hard. There are probably more people who start something and quit than people who quit because they fail.

Be Honest with Yourself

I spent a lot of my life telling lies. Lies to myself. Lies to other people and lies about other people. When I used to get into fights I blamed other people, even if it was my fault. Later on I would have these great thoughts but nothing came of them. I can't tell you the number of books I had in my head but never wrote. Basically I was lying to myself. If you want to make something happen, you need to be almost brutally honest about yourself. And what you need to ask yourself first is, 'Am I a quitter?' I certainly was.

If you listen carefully to people, you will notice that they are very good at giving reasons for their 'bad luck'. It's because of the upbringing, the schooling, the boss, the partner. Or there aren't enough hours in the day. I'm of the opinion that these limiting beliefs are a way of avoiding the simple truth—some people just don't want it enough. It's a lot easier to sit in your cosy armchair and tell the world that you didn't get the breaks, than it is to get up and do something about it.

I reckon that many people find it hard to stick at something in today's world. That's partly because our society is a more shifting one now. Thirty or 40 years ago, when employers were more loyal and employees had a job for life, people found it easier to commit to something for the long term. You started at the bottom and you slowly but surely worked your way to the top. You knew it would take years to get there, but that was just the way things were. Many people who are at the top of companies today worked their way up.

The problem now is that we want it instantly. We live in a world where everything is—or seems to be—at our fingertips. Just click a button and you can have it. You don't have to wait until the news comes on television. You can read it as it happens on the internet. You can order your shopping online and use the red button on your digital TV. Instead of waiting for someone to call you, you can send a text, email or instant message to remind them. We have 'instant cook' rice when normal rice takes only 15 minutes to cook, but suddenly that's far too long. The whole idea is that there is no waiting.

The danger with this is that everyone starts to think in a short-term way. Kids go to university and leave thinking, 'I'm going to get a big job in the City now and get rich.' People are lining up to go on reality TV shows because they believe they can be famous and make a lot of money very quickly. Why work for it when you can make a monkey of yourself and get rewarded more quickly? Cosmetic surgery is popular because women (and men) think they can get rid of all those years of overeating, smoking, drinking and being lazy just by going under the knife.

We are all in a hurry. Look at people waiting for a lift. They might be waiting for only a minute instead of 20 seconds, but that extra 40 seconds puts a scowl on their face. And yet, despite this instant world of ours, the real successes do not come without real effort. Hard work will always be involved, even if it doesn't look like it is. If you really want something you will have to put in the work. As they say, success is ambition with a finish line.

Can You Handle the Hard Graft?

There will always be people who make it look easy. You met them at school, the ones who breezed through exams or made all the sports teams without looking like they tried. Sure, there are people who are 'natural' but don't forget they're not good at everything. Okay, there are a few freaks in the world who can turn their hands to anything and succeed, but you would be lucky to know more than one in your lifetime. Because that's what they are—freaks of nature. What is interesting about these 'natural' stars is that so many of them don't amount to much, because they've had it easy all their lives. They have never had to try hard to do much, so they stop trying. I know people who could have had it all but now they are fully grown adults with no purpose, no personal success in life. It is often these people who never reach their potential.

Have you thought about those other people, at school, the ones who were not 'naturals' but simply tried harder? Quite often the people who have to make an extra effort to succeed, do better in life than the so-called 'naturals'. The fact that they feel they are starting from behind seems to motivate them to try even harder. It's rather like people with physical disabilities. A man who cannot walk because of a car accident will become even more determined to live a full life. This is part of the human spirit and what makes it wonderful.

I am not a natural winner. You only have to look at my background to see that. I spent a large part of my life—until my 40s—being a loser until I decided that I wanted to make something of myself. Once I did, I had to figure out how to do it. I want to win, and I know that to do that I have to work harder and put in more energy than most. For example, I am not organised. I do not like to make lists. I prefer big ideas to small details. So when it came to dealing with all those things for the magazine I could easily have said, 'I don't do this stuff. I'm not good at it and I've never been good at it. Find someone else.' But I couldn't. I had to get in there and figure out how to do it.

It took a huge effort for me to turn my brain into something that had the patience to cope with details. Things like figures and budgets are not so much hard as slow-going. You have to keep cutting and fitting until you get things right. I had to learn how to do that from the beginning. I had to learn the computer program. Once I began to understand the budgets, I was really pleased with myself. In fact, I remember sitting with two accountants and a bookkeeper, looking at our monthly accounts. Something wasn't right and it was me who spotted it, not them.

What it comes down to is that, if you want to succeed, then you have to knuckle down and work damn hard until you crack it. Imagine there is a big heavy door in front of you. You can't open it. You have a sledgehammer, so you keep taking swings at it. You keep on hitting it until it breaks. So after 99 hits, the door finally gives way. Do you think that it was that last blow that did the job? No way. Trouble is, most people won't reach that point, because at about the 50th swing of the sledgehammer they'll say that it's just too hard and they're never going to do it.

Get in Properly or Get Out

I think you need to want to win. If you think you only need to get almost there, but not the whole way, you won't even get off the ground. The field I work in means that I need to have a 'do or die' attitude. You cannot have a halfway attitude to the question of poverty and the poor. You have to have drive, energy and imagination. I am not here to make friends among homeless people or organisations. I am here to make things better, and try and change a system that isn't working.

My message to you is put your money down where it matters or get out of the game. If you're playing at it, you may as well not be doing it. If you think that your big idea will carry you through without effort, then you may as well stop reading now. Maybe your idea will turn out to be crap, but before that happens you will have made the effort of your life to make sure it isn't. And that's more than most people in this world have done.

Remember

- Believe in yourself and your ideas. Are you in or out?
- Make sure you're in the right race and that you're equipped for it. If you're not, get out of it and into the right one.
- Don't turn and run at the first sign of problems. This is when winners show what they're made of.
- If it's not working, accept that you need to change something. Stick with what you're doing until you have done everything you can to make it work.
- Get out of the mindset that you are not 'naturally' made to do what you are doing.
- Everything you are doing will add up and one day it will add up to success.

Chapter Seven

Take Your Failure Personally

It's easy to get sucked in by the countless articles and books that tell you that failure is not personal. They would have you believe it's not that much to do with you. It's the weather, the planets, fate and, of course, the government. Anything and anyone but you. Well, I'm sorry but the truth is that your failure is personal. Failure has to matter to you because otherwise you will just walk away and not learn from what has happened. And that will get in the way of your success.

Failing is a big part of the learning process that we must go through in order to advance ourselves in life. The challenge isn't in the process of failing or making a mistake. It's in how we behave and move on when we make mistakes. Many of the people who have done very well in our society have failed many more times than they have succeeded. The only difference between them and you is that they kept at it until they found a way to make it work. You have to take failure personally and it has to matter. If it doesn't, it means you don't care enough to make it work.

You Are Allowed to Fail

Sure, failure can crush you if you take it the wrong way, but that will only happen if you think mistakes are bad. They are not if you learn from them. It is only when you turn your back and pretend they never happened or they were someone else's fault that it becomes a problem. There is a saying that smart people learn from their mistakes, smarter people learn from other people's mistakes, and the smartest people learn from smart people's mistakes.

However, it's not easy to fail today. The big businesses that run our world do not accept failure. For them, only pure success will do. To succeed on their terms, you must reach every goal and never, *ever* make a mistake that you can't hide or blame on someone else. They won't say that, of course. Instead they will say things like, 'We expect our employees to perform to the highest standards.' But you know that what they mean is, 'We're watching you and don't you dare fail or we'll replace you.' Imagine the stress and terror people go through in a workplace like that. A place where people are always trying to cover up mistakes or wildly pointing the finger at someone else to shift the blame. A place where staff turnover is rapid as people rise high then fall just as quickly from grace.

The lying, cheating and hiding of problems are all results of a culture that does not permit failure.

As children, we hear failure defined in so many ways—being poor, not having certain things, not being popular or good looking. Some of you may even have felt like failures because your parents said you were. All of this sets up 'failure' as a dirty word. And so we start to fear it, and we avoid doing things that might make us feel like a failure.

Everyone likes to succeed. That's normal. The problem comes when fear of failure is so great that you cannot accept that mistakes will happen. Then you are doomed. Instead of looking for the best, most creative solution, you will settle for something safe that has less risk attached to it. Thank God there are people who are willing to risk it all and fail, or we would not have much greatness in the world. Sure, things would happen but we would be surrounded by dullness. Good ideas would never see the light of day. It's a fact that the more creative you are, the more errors you will make. The only way that will not happen is if you don't put your best efforts into something, but settle for something average. To my mind that's not a great way to live. It's only half-living. And that in itself is failure.

Learning to accept failure as part of the process of success is vital. In fact, the more failures you have and the more quickly they happen, the quicker you will learn. Why? Because each time you fail you move closer to success. You get on a bike, you fall off. You get on, you fall off again. After a while you stop falling off. Success! Of course, if you decide to give up halfway through it will take you longer to get there.

As children, we are more prepared to make mistakes. Somehow it seems a natural part of our lives. As we get older we become more cautious, partly because of what our parents, teachers and others tell us. We decide that we don't want to fail. So we take the safe way forward, dream of what we could have done, and admire those people who sail around the world, climb mountains, set up businesses on a shoestring and let themselves fall in love. 'How do they do it?' we ask ourselves. Simple. They focus on their goals instead of their fears.

Failure is the Flip Side of Success

Failure comes at a high cost because the rewards are high. But don't let that put you off. You need to hug failure as much as you do success, because your attitude towards failure is directly related to your success. When I started *The Big Issue* I wasn't doing it to get rid of homelessness, as some people seem to think. That would have been setting myself up to fail. I have always said that I started the magazine to get rid of homelessness in *some* people's lives. As I pointed out earlier, your dreams have to fit with reality. In other words, they have to be just beyond your grasp, not up there in the Milky Way. I was prepared to fail but only as part of the path to success.

In the past I would have run away from failure or put it on to someone else. I once did a book that was being published by a small business I was a part of. It failed. The reason was that I did not take the marketing seriously enough. I left it to a man who had a serious drinking problem. And when it failed I knew who was to blame. I certainly wasn't going to blame myself, was I? Yet it was my fault. I knew he had a serious drinking problem and I let it all happen.

With *The Big Issue*, however, I knew I was responsible for the project. This time I couldn't pass the buck if something went wrong. Instead, I would stand there and put it right. A few years ago it was obvious that we would soon hit the rocks. The marketplace had changed and we were losing big money. The general feeling was that I had lost the plot and was unable to direct the company on the right road. We needed to reduce our costs, so I got rid of some people and brought in some others. I made the cuts we needed. I may well have led the magazine wrongly, but I knew I was the only one who could set it right.

I never asked myself what would happen if *The Big Issue* failed. At the risk of sounding a little too airy fairy even for my own liking, I think my attitude helped. I wasn't afraid. I wasn't afraid to hire the wrong people, so I hired the right ones. I wasn't afraid of not knowing things, so I learned them very quickly. I wasn't afraid of what people would say about us, so I won them over. I wasn't afraid of people looking down on me if I failed. That didn't happen. And when things came along to trip us up, I was able to deal with them.

It is said that Thomas Edison 'failed' at his attempts to invent the light bulb over 10,000 times. When he was asked how he kept going, he said he simply believed that what he had in fact done was discover 10,000 ways *not* to invent the light bulb! He never looked upon any of his attempts as failures. Instead, he saw them as a chance to learn. We all know that success is how we are measured. But within each success are all the failures lined up out of sight. They are there to remind us how we did it and to let us know that nothing comes easily. Do not ignore them or your success may be short-lived.

We hear a lot about being positive. Maybe we also need to recognise that the negative parts of our lives and experiences have just as important a role to play in finding success, in work and in life. If we are able to do that, we can take responsibility for our failures. Balance counts more than you think. Some sharpness must season the sweetest dish. A little selfishness is valuable even in the most caring person. And a little failure is essential to understand success.

Remember

- Accept that you are going to make mistakes.
- Accept that you are going to learn from your mistakes.
- To be afraid of failure is to only half live your life.
- The more failures you have, the quicker you will learn!
- Overcome your fear of failure by focusing on your goals instead of your fears.
- If you try to do something and it

doesn't work out, you've still succeeded. You've learned that what you did was not the way to get what it was you were after.

Chapter Eight

Look Outside Yourself

Many of the books that deal in 'positive thinking' will tell you that you should never compare yourself to others. They will tell you it will only make you unhappy and not help you to achieve your goals. There will always be someone above you and someone better than you. In other words, your self-esteem will take a pounding. I agree that it's stupid to compare your lifestyle with someone else's. That is not positive. But, if sticking your head out of the window to see what others are doing will improve your chances of success then you need to do it. And do it with a clear head so that you can learn from it.

Even though your project might feel very personal, there is always something to be gained from looking at what others are doing. This is not about competing. It's about learning to compare yourself with others in a way that helps you improve your own efforts and, therefore, your chances of success. You can't do that by looking inwards.

You Can Always Improve

We are often advised that our success is personal, that it is just down to us. However, it can often be useful to compare yourself with someone who is doing the same thing as you. Someone you admire or even someone you don't admire in the same field. If you are hell bent on succeeding at what you have chosen to do, whether it's market a new beauty product, build better sheds or clean cars, then you need to know what other people are doing right. And what they are not doing right.

How do you know how good you are if you don't know how good other people are?

I am always looking at what other people are doing with their lives and their businesses. Without that I feel I am self-obsessed and, frankly, a bit stupid. It's a very nice thought that you can measure success by your inner peace and calm, but I want more than that. I want to know that part of my success is that I have left no stone unturned in my desire to improve and change. And that means I need to compare.

Now let's get one thing clear. When I say *compare* I don't mean *compete*. To compare yourself is to stand back and take an honest look at what you are doing against what others are doing in the same area. That other ice-cream van down the beach—how come there are always more people in his line? Is it because he is doing something better or is he simply slow at serving? See what I mean. This sort of thing helps you to ask questions about yourself that you might not think of otherwise. It helps make you better.

Learn to Be the Observer

Standing back and watching might seem like a really lazy thing to do, especially if you're trying to get something off the ground. It's natural to think that, unless you spend every day actually at your desk or in your workshop doing something, then you're not doing anything at all. That is wrong and I'll tell you why.

Have you ever noticed that when you're at a family or even a work gathering, there are people who don't say much at all? They are not shy, stupid or even bored. They're very clever. What they do is stand back, watch and listen to everyone else instead of throwing their own noise into the middle. When they do say something, it is usually spot on. The quality of what they say is far better than everyone else in the room. These are the people who understand their rivals, their bosses and their staff. They are the people who are best placed to see problems before they happen. And they are often the people who suggest ways to solve problems. They are the quiet achievers.

Most of us are in the habit of not looking, of not hearing, of not noticing. It's a bad habit that's hard to break, but it will pay off if you can break it. Call it observing, call it spying if you want, but you need to practise it. Focus on one kind of event or challenge to start with. For example, you might want to watch people in meetings. Don't say anything like you normally do. Just see how others do it. I bet you learn something.

Observing people is often the most

difficult thing to do. You feel passive. You feel as if you are not being yourself. But without a good deal of standing back and watching, I would be lost. Without looking at how people get it right, or get it wrong, you have only your experience to rely on.

Good observing is like borrowing other people's experience. It's as though by good observing you learn how to avoid other people's mistakes, but at the same time make yourself open for learning. It's like sneaking knowledge from other people, but in a good way.

One day I went down to the headquarters of The Body Shop to have a meeting with Anita Roddick, who was a good friend. We were planning *The Big Issue* launch. I sat in a room of 20 people and listened. I listened to people who had experience in launching campaigns. These people had many years of experience. I made notes. I carefully wrote down the names of people I could talk to later, such as the bloke who started a newspaper for council tenants.

I was so careful and behaving so out of character that the room fell silent. I had to say something. I praised the contributions. I told people how good it had been.

Anita, who knew me of old, rang me later. 'What were you doing at the meeting today?' she asked. I said, 'I was just listening and learning.' She laughed. Then she said something magical. 'Maybe you are making yourself useful after all.'

That was Anita's way of saying something good. Yes, she was right. Listening and observing was a big key to success.

I Am Still Learning

Many people ask me to speak to them because they think I am a success. Yet I know I have only touched the tip of the iceberg and have much to learn. A lot of the time I am looking for a new opportunity to show even more people what I can do. I made a TV programme in 2006 that was quite a big deal for me. It was on Channel 4 and it meant that I reached people I might not normally reach. Before I did it I had many chances to see how other people did the same sort of thing. That helped me work out how to make my programme good. In the end they said it was a good piece of TV, but I know I can do better. I knew it straight after I'd finished. But that's okay. That's what it's all about. Watching and learning.

Remember

- Don't be afraid to compare yourself to others and learn from them.

- Make it a habit to ask questions of yourself.
- Be humble enough to ask questions of others.
- Learn the art of being an observer and you will be surprised how much you see that you didn't see before.
- Let someone else do the talking and listen to them.
- Don't make the mistake of thinking you know everything. Then you stop learning.

Chapter Nine

Recognise that Success *is* Always Shifting

What do you think success is? Be careful before you answer. I'm not asking you what the fruits of your success are. I don't want to know about money, cars and glamorous women and men. I'm asking what you would define as success. When do you think you have reached it? Is it when you complete what you set out to do? For example, if success is about finishing something, that would mean I was a success by setting up *The Big Issue*. But I don't see it like that. I see myself as on a continual road to success.

That's because success does not stand still. It is always shifting. One thing you will find—as I did—is that once you have reached a goal you may not want to rest on your laurels. Instead, you feel ready to take on more. One of the great things about success is that, as well as developing you as a person, it gives you energy and confidence to take on new things.

Success Can Be a Strange Feeling

The road to success will probably be full of rejection, pain, hard work, as well as many other things. In the end, though, you will feel like you control your part of the world, no matter how small it is. You will feel proud of yourself for getting past all of those obstacles and for reaching your goals.

Then you might ask yourself, 'Shouldn't I be jumping around or something?' Not really. The thing is, you've probably worked towards this goal for so long that your life and attitude have changed along with it.

Since you started you have changed from a negative person, who perhaps had no idea of what they could do, into one who realised they could achieve a great deal. And so your expectations of yourself have changed. The good and bad news is that you probably now have higher expectations of yourself to live up to.

Some people might say this is a sign of not being happy with yourself. That is total rubbish. It is in our nature to want to change and improve things. It's evident in our desire to paint our walls a different colour, shift our furniture around and change our hair style. Okay, if you start shifting the furniture around every week you have a serious problem, but you know what I mean. I don't think there's anything wrong with asking what is going to happen next as long as you do it in a positive frame of mind. For instance, if you went back to college after 15 years, it would be good to say,

'Wow! I passed my exams. Next year I'm going to see if I can get higher marks.' The problem starts when you say, 'Well, I passed, but I didn't do that well. I'm not that good at this, am I?' It's all in how you look at things. Remember what we said at the beginning—you have to keep your optimism.

It can be hard. Success is often followed by the blues. There is a period of celebration after reaching a milestone, but this is often short. There are hugs, handshakes and pats on the back and then what? You go home, sit in a chair and suddenly feel lost. Plus you are really tired. You've worked long and hard to get where you are and given up quite a lot in the process. The push for a goal excites us, and we work harder and better than we thought we could. This is draining physically, mentally and emotionally.

The thing is, life is like that. Very few things will ever match up totally to what you expect. If you remember that, then you will be okay. If it matches up to even 80 per cent of what you thought, then be happy with that. The point is there is no particular way you are supposed to feel after reaching a goal. Your life will not be perfect because you have reached this point. That doesn't mean you shouldn't enjoy what you have already achieved. It's not just the goal you've reached, but the hurdles you've overcome along the way. Don't fall into the trap of thinking about what you didn't achieve. I could tell you about a thousand things I wished I'd done with *The Big Issue*, things I could have done better, but I recognised that I could use that knowledge later on. In the end I got there and discovered new things about myself along the way.

One evening I was in a West End club when a famous writer was talking to a famous actor. I walked past. One of them put their hand out and congratulated me for *The Big Issue*. So I stopped and stood with them at the bar. We had more things to say to each other. Then the famous writer said, 'It's a pity the magazine is full of so much crap.' The actor and I looked at each other and then at the writer. He carried on, 'I had high hopes for *The Big Issue*. But you know it's a great idea, a great help but a great letdown.'

I did not defend myself and the magazine. I stood and looked at the bloke. I realised he might have been saying something that could have been put in a more positive way. Everything can be put in a more positive way if you think about it. He might have been useful. But he wasn't. His negative mind could have poisoned me. I struggled not to let it.

It was a bit of a wakeup call. The next morning I went into work early. I got the editions out on the floor and looked at them. This was success. I could see it on the floor in front of me. Each week we had hard-hitting stuff mixed with lighter material. We also now had the homeless selling hundreds of thousands of copies.

We were a success. A big success. But we were also a general publication so we had to appeal to everyone. Most magazines don't have to do that. They just have to appeal to certain audiences, such as men who like computers or women who like fashion. Not us. We had to have wide appeal ranging from city gent to poor student.

But I still had to contend with a reality. It was not the big, tough publication I wanted it to be. It wasn't the one that the world turned to weekly for that bit of reality. In a way we could only be as good as our readers.

But now after 16 years we are changing again. We are beginning to raise issues where we lead the public in their thinking. That is a good thing. I don't mind that the writer said those things. It made me look harder at my magazine.

Recognise All that Has Come to You

Because of my work with the homeless and in setting up *The Big Issue*, I am often asked to speak to groups of people. I have spoken to governments, to the police and to law-makers. I am just a bloke without a formal education. I did not learn how to make speeches. I am not a natural public speaker. There was always a danger that I would come off looking bad, and that would undermine the work I was trying to do with the homeless. On the other hand, I knew that if I could do it, I would get positive publicity for *The Big Issue* and for the homeless. So I made an effort to become better at it. At the risk of sounding big-headed, I am now pretty good.

They say success breeds success. I would put it another way. Success increases your chances of having another success. If you manage to get that West End musical on stage and it works, then there is a greater chance that people will trust you to do another.

One of the big side-effects of success is in your own personal development. I know that, as I have spread *The Big Issue* all over the world and reached more and more people, I have changed. I feel more respect for myself. I get more joy from what I do. It is less like hard work and more like a way of living. I have lost many of the worries that go with starting something that you don't know will work. I have a greater depth to my thinking. I have greater control of my anger. I am a more useful man. I waste less time. And I meet people who are themselves more useful.

Then there are my energy levels which have gone through the roof. I now have more energy, even though I am a decade and a half older than when I first started *The Big Issue*. Where does that energy come from? It comes from the kind of direction and focus that comes with success. I am not wasting it on unproductive things. Now that I have a better idea of what I am doing, I can reap some of the positive rewards of my effort and take the driver's seat a bit more often. I know that I matter as a person and that people want to listen to what I have to say.

As for money, well, let me say it once and for all—money is a by-product of success. It is not the success itself. Doing what you enjoy and being happy with your choices are more important than just doing something for money. Of course, if you are happy and working hard at something that happens to be money-making, then chances are that you will do very well.

Remember

- You may feel low and let down after reaching certain goals. Be prepared.
- Success may not feel like a big deal when you get there because you have adjusted to what you are doing.
- Success does not stand still. Be aware that, as you move forward, it also keeps shifting.
- Success in one area often opens doors in another.
- Success helps to develop you as a person and makes you more confident about trying new things in other areas of your life.
- Money is a by-product of success. It is not the success itself.

Chapter Ten

No-one Can Unlock the Door Except You

If you've read this far, chances are you have found something to interest you. I like to think that I've told it how it is, that I haven't sugar-coated anything for you. At the same time I hope I've given you the feeling that things are not hard to achieve once you know what you are doing. At this point many books would tell you to bounce out of bed and start your new life or path of action straight away. I'm not going to do that.

As I've said all along, success is a series of steps—often small ones—that get you to where you're going. It's like one of those gigantic jigsaws that you start and keep doing over a period of time. Some of you will give up and throw the whole thing into the air. Others will go backwards and forwards, putting pieces in as they go along.

Remember, I didn't really have any idea or direction until I was 45. I don't want you to think that means that up till now you've wasted your life, because you haven't. Everything I'd done until that time—good and bad—brought me to the point where I could start *The Big Issue*. That's an important point—your negative experiences are as important as your positive ones in building your success, and it's true in every area of your life.

I hope that I have given you starting points to make you think about your life. I'm not some guru who has a magic key to it all. I'm just a bloke who knows that focus and hard work will get you somewhere and make you a happier person. Nothing I have written in the book is out of your reach, but it will require you to study yourself perhaps harder than you ever have before.

Think . . .

Figure out what you're good at and what you can do in the real world. What are your skills? What are your dreams? How can you make them match? You may have to be a bit cold about this. And you may have to water down or fine-tune a dream to match your skills. It's good to aim high but make sure you've got the arrow to shoot that far. You need to have a firm idea of what you are going for. If you are too airy fairy, it just won't work. Ideally, it will play to your strengths. And if you've read this far, you will have realised that you have some.

Part of thinking is believing. You need to believe in yourself, no matter what others think of you. When I said fight for your optimism, I meant that it is a fight. Every day your biggest enemy won't be your own limits. It will be the people you know well and don't know well who will play on your mind. They will tell you that you can't do it, that you are stupid and that you will be unhappy. Use their words to make you fight even harder.

Act ...

You could start tomorrow. Or the next day. Or the day after that. But you could also start today. There is very rarely a right time to do anything, whether it's starting a business, moving house or falling in love. Something won't be quite right. People who are successful in life tend to take their chances. Not in a stupid way, but with an awareness of the risks they are taking. Then they jump in. They trust their judgement and so should you.

At the same time they look at

things with a cool eye and an even cooler head. It's easy to be a dreamer, and it's also very nice to think you have these great ideas. But, unless you can make them work in real life, they are not great ideas. And unless you can sell them to the people who need to believe in them—whether it's your family or people at work—then they're useless. Don't try to win them over by making it sound all big and wonderful. You'll have more chance if you show that you've thought about the small stuff, the details that matter.

I've talked quite a bit about taking small steps. That's because success itself is a series of small steps that add up. It's not about shouting or arm waving. It's about taking on the small things first, the things you can do easily so that you get something under your belt. When you have that, you will also have the confidence to take on more. Trust me on that one.

And don't think you have to prove yourself to everybody. You are only out to meet goals that you have set for yourself.

Work

The world owes you nothing, but it will give you something if you put in the effort. If you want it badly enough, then you should be excited by what you are doing. Even though it may seem hard you have to keep going. Remember, there are more people who quit because they can't go the distance than people who fail.

Learning to accept failure as part of the process of success is vital. The more failures you have and the more quickly they happen, the quicker you will learn. Why? Because each time you fail you move closer to success. Failure is really the stops we make on our journey to reflect and think.

Remember that other people fail.

You can learn as much from watching and listening to them as you can by doing. Don't be afraid to look outside and see what the rest of the world is doing. Learn to be a quiet observer. The ability to watch and learn is as good a use of your time as any.

Succeed

What is success after all? It is many things to many people. Perhaps you will find it isn't what you thought. Or maybe you will wish for more. That's okay, as long as you stop to smell the roses and say, 'Gosh, I did all right.' Allow yourself to enjoy what you have done. Even if you don't think it was that big a deal in the end or you could have done better, just remember this—you did it when many people were just sitting around talking about it. Be proud.

I have experience with success.

When you don't have it you want it desperately. Then, when you get a taste of it, you realise you need more than success. You need to feel you are doing something useful for yourself, for others. To me, a sense of achievement is what success is all about. I have never made lots of money. I suppose that's because it has never been my number one priority. Plus—and I'm not just saying this—I have met too many people who think their money makes them special. It doesn't. If I have admired them, it's not because of their money.

For me, the ultimate key to success is to value your achievements, and to value the people around you—family and friends, workmates and the people you work for. I don't have an employer but I do work for homeless people. Only when I can look them in the eye can I say I have found success. But then I want more. I'm a greedy sod. I want to see more people get out of a life of poverty, crime and need.

I recently met up with a very rich friend of mine. All he could talk about was the trees he was planting. The money only made sense to him when he turned it into trees. Now isn't that funny. Money is made out of paper, which is made out of trees. He was returning his money to the trees where it all started. Good on him.

If you want to be the biggest and the best, then good luck. But don't turn your thirst into a boring quest for status.

Go look at the trees. They'll be here when you've gone.

About the Author

John Bird is the founder and editor of *The Big Issue*, a news and current affairs magazine launched in September 1991. It is written by professional journalists and sold on the streets by homeless vendors looking to break the cycle of poverty and homelessness. Vendors buy the magazine at a wholesale rate and sell it, keeping the profit for themselves. They are self-employed and encouraged to be responsible for handling their earnings.

John was born into a London Irish family in a slum-ridden part of Notting Hill just after the Second World War. Homeless at five, in an orphanage between seven and ten, he began to fail over and over again in every area of his life. From the age of ten onwards he was shoplifting, house-breaking and stealing whatever he could lay his hands on. Vandalism and arson were also among the crimes he committed.

In his late twenties, and after several prison sentences, John became involved in politics. He also fathered three children, became a printer and successfully ran his own small business. At the age of 45, his many life experiences enabled him to start production of *The Big Issue*.

He has spent the last 14 years in charge of the development of *The Big Issue*—which is now an international movement—providing opportunities for people facing homelessness to help themselves. It forges partnerships with social entrepreneurs to launch businesses for social change in cities worldwide. Setting up street papers to help socially excluded people is central to this.

John Bird was awarded the MBE for 'services to homeless people' by Her Majesty the Queen in June

1995. He is a Fellow of John Moore's University, Liverpool, a Visiting Professor at Lincoln University, and a Doctor of Letters at Oxford Brookes University. In 2003, he was chosen by the Queen as one of the top Most Important Pioneers in Her Majesty's Reign. In 2004, he received from the United Nations a Scroll of Excellence for his international work in poverty, presented by the President of Kenya at the Habitat Celebration in Nairobi. In the same year he also won a public vote by BBC London as London's Living Legend, beating people such as Terence Conran, Barbara Windsor and Linford Christie.